The Right Season

Poetry for Jamaican and Caribbean Children

Cecile Jarrett

iUniverse, Inc.
Bloomington

The Right Season
Poetry for Jamaican and Caribbean Children

iUniverse books may be ordered through booksellers or by contacting:

iUniverse
1663 Liberty Drive
Bloomington, IN 47403
www.iuniverse.com
1-800-Authors (1-800-288-4677)

ISBN: 978-1-4502-8805-7 (sc)
ISBN: 978-1-4502-8806-4 (ebk)

Printed in the United States of America

iUniverse rev. date: 09/13/2011

Contents

Endorsement

On behalf of the Jamaica Independent Schools' Association, I am pleased to endorse this children's anthology, *The Right Season*, written by Cecile A. Jarrett.

The Jamaica Independent Schools' Association is always happy when our own teachers produce material that is relevant to our heritage and culture for children. This collection of poems will be a tremendously refreshing contribution to children's literature in Jamaica and the Caribbean.

It is certain that students will benefit greatly from reading, learning and reciting these poems with their rhythmic patterns and colourful language. I therefore encourage teachers and parents to use this anthology as resource material in their schools and homes.

Renee Rattry, President 2008

Foreword

For Our Children's Children

Here are some songs
For our children
Here are songs to tell them how
To live much better
Here, there and everywhere

This song will help
To make their world
A wholesome place
Will show to them
Their greatness
As a race
Will lift their pride
From deep inside

Good deeds today
Miracles tomorrow
Bringing joy
Healing sorrow

Here's a song
Of love of life
Of keeping
Drugs, violence and strife
Away from self
And other children's life

And…
Here's another song
Of caring for the environment
Lofty hills, valleys deep
The sucancobanas' lush growth
Sea sands glow white in sunlight

Songs go on …
About the disabled
The less fortunate child
Songs to make them happy
Songs to make them smile
Songs to keep them singing
All the while

Songs, songs, songs
For independent thinking
Creativity and gain
Of freedom
From indiscipline
Fear and
Needless pain

Songs about today
Songs about tomorrow
A promising new dawn
That will bring less harm

I am writing
For the children
Generations to come

Dedication

This anthology is dedicated to Salome, who in 2005, inspired me to start writing for children and who enjoys reading the work; Jonathan, my consummate listener and critic; Celeste, the quiet but absorbed listener; all my other grandchildren; the children of Jamaica, the Caribbean and the world.

  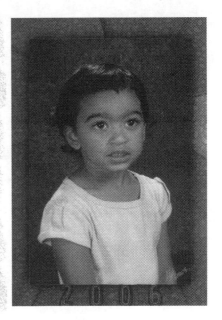

Acknowledgments

Although many persons have contributed to the creation and development of this anthology, I owe a debt of gratitude to those persons named below because of their personal interest in the work and quality time that they invested in helping to bring it to completion:

Mrs. Carmen Tipling, Communications Consultant and playwright who made the time to critique the work, recommend the name for anthology and pushed me to have the poems published;

Dr. Renee Rattry, past principal of St Andrew Preparatory School and past president of The Jamaica Independent Schools Association—JISA, for endorsing the anthology as literature suitable for Jamaican/Caribbean schools;

The principal and staff of Lalyce Gray Basic School for giving me permission to pilot the work in their institution;

The principal and staff of Porter's Centre for Knowledge for selecting a group of students to listen to the reading of the Ackee, Pattee and Dumplin Poems and reacting to it;

Dr. Paulette McGregor, staff and students of Liguanea Preparatory School for their positive critical feedback;

Mrs. Jennease Green Guy, Art Teacher—Stella Maris Preparatory, for illustrating the characters—Ackee, Pattee, Dumpling and Bevie Bee; and critiquing the cover design;

Mr. Wittel Richardson, Nikki LaChambre and Master Jonathan Nairne for their contribution of photographs that have been used to enrich the work;

Dr. Faithlyn Wilson, Principal and Literacy Specialist—El Instituto de Mandevilla for her frank feedback and introduction to the work;

Mr. Norbert Smith, farmer, for allowing me to include a photograph of his vegetable garden in the anthology;

Miss Janice Jarrett, Ms. Nadine Walker-Wright, Mr. Renaldo Jarrett and Miss Sheraine Lumsden, IT teacher – Stella Maris Preparatory School, for their willing assistance with the word processing challenges that I faced occasionally;

Ms Betty Black of **All Spice** magazine for directing me to the Government of Jamaica, GOJ, web page to find a free picture of a Jamaican green parrot;

Mrs. Janilee Abrikian of PALS Jamaica for her encouraging response to the poem, "PALS", and for allowing the use of Perky Parrot's picture to illustrate the poem;

The Archer family for the gift of the praying girl and their assurance of the artist's permission to use the work;

Mr. Denis Dale, photographer, for his permission to use a photograph from his Gallery of Jamaican Scenes to illustrate the poem, "Our Environment", based on the condition that he be given a copy of the publication;

Mrs. Katrine Smith of Visual and Performing Arts Jamaican (VPAJ), for critiquing the cover and recommending changes that are more appealing to children, to the back cover;

Ms. Nadine Walker Wright for her support and the quality time that she invested in proof reading the print-ready draft; thank you Nadine for your generosity, positive attitude and thoroughness;

Liana Wright for allowing her mother, Nadine Walker Wright, to spend time away from home to assist me by proof reading the draft and for her genuine feedback on Sucancobana and other poems.

Introduction

The Right Season, an anthology written by Cecile Jarrett is an excellent contribution to Children's Literature. Written specifically for children in Jamaica and the wider Caribbean, Poet Cecile Jarrett has managed to effectively combine the unique experiences and strong feelings of our children with the rhythmic patterns necessary to help them explore and discover language as well as their distinct Jamaican/Caribbean culture.

Cecile has managed to put together the whole range of poetic elements in her work—lyric, narrative, and dramatic to help children of all ages connect with the text as they are presented with opportunities to laugh, use comprehension strategies such as visualizing, predicting, asking questions, and connecting background knowledge, whilst discovering the variety in the structure of our language. ***The Right Season*** makes a good companion to our integrated approach to teaching and learning at the early childhood and primary levels.

It is clear that Cecile has had many of the experiences of which she writes, hence the richness and authenticity of the ideas and feelings which are conveyed in each poem. Her poetry sings! Every child in Jamaica and the wider Caribbean should experience this season—it's the Right Season to read her work.

Dr. Faithlyn Wilson. Principal, El Instituto de Mandevilla, **2011 Feriar 18**

Glossary of Jamaican Terms

Word/Term	Standard English Usage
A learn	Are learning
Ackee	The ackee is fruit grown in Jamaica. It is said to have been brought to the island from West Africa during slavery. Ackee trees grow to height of about thirty feet and produce a bright red or orange fruit— the ackee. When fully mature the pod with the fleshy bright yellow fruit bursts open to reveal its contents; the yellow fruit with its shiny black seed. It is this soft yellow fruit that is used with cod or salted fish in Jamaica's national dish— ackee and salt fish. In the work the poet recognizes the popularity of the ackee through the friendly but slightly mischievous character, Ackee, friend of Patee and Dumplin.
Bogle	Paul Bogle, one of Jamaica's seven National Heroes
Dash in	Throw quickly or place hurriedly
Dat	that
De	the

Dem	them
Dis	this
Dumplin	Dumpling without the final letter. One of Ackee's two friends and also a popular food item made from wheat flour. In Jamaica, dumplings are made in a variety of ways. The wheat flour may be mixed with cornmeal, whole wheat, cassava or any starchy tuber. It may be fried or boiled. Fried dumplings are also called Johnny Cakes and are often consumed as the main carbohydrate with ackee and salt fish, Jamaica's national dish.
Dung	Down
Eena	In or Into
Englan'	England
Fi	For
Gwaan	going on
Homan	Woman
I of the Storm	The fury/nature of a hurricane
Jahgga	A name coined for an imaginable, ancient, wise and mysterious Crayfish.
Jah	is a Rastafarian title for God and Jahgga is endowed with ancient wisdom that comes from God himself.

Lignum Vitae	The Lignum Vitae is a small evergreen tree that abounds in Jamaica. Lignum Vitae means tree of life because it has many medicinal uses. Its blue flower is Jamaica's national flower.
Man marina	Men's merinos or men's cotton under-shirt
Mek	make
'Merica	America; the USA
Meuse	A small district in the parish of St. Catherine. The district is believed to have been named after a small river found there. The Meuse is a major river in Europe.
PALS	An acronym for Peace and Love in Schools/Society—a not-for-profit foundation in Jamaica that promotes non-violent solutions nationally and within the school.
Pattee	A playful character created from patty—a Jamaican pastry that contains a variety of spicy savoury fillings and baked inside a flaky shell. It is a very popular lunchtime meal for many Jamaicans. In this anthology, Ackee, Pattee and Dumplin are best of friends.
Piano key-board friend	A friend with light complexion- a fair-skinned person.
Pickney	Children
Posse	Good friends
Sucancobana	The name created for the plant on the front cover— a comical representation of the tropical plants: sugar cane (sucan), coconut (co) and banana (bana), a depiction of the right season

Tin pan	A container made from tin that was originally used to keep patties warm. It was a very popular container among patty sellers in the 1950's and 1960's. Today it is an artifact.
t'ings	things
wi	we

Small Steps

Poems for 2-5 year olds or Nursery to Upper Kindergarten

One Two

One, two
I love you

Three, four
We'll have more

Five, six
Don't play tricks

Seven, eight
See a plate

Nine, ten
Let us say it all over again

One-2-Three

One, two, three
Stay with me

Four, five, six
We can mix

Seven, eight and nine
We are standing in a line.

One, Two, Three, Four

One, two, three, four
Why are you
On the floor
Five, six, seven, eight
Why are you
Always late
Nine, ten, eleven twelve
Is this a boy or an elf?

Busy as a Hive

One, two
Three, four, five
I'm as busy as a hive

Six, seven,
Eight, nine, ten
We are counting
Bees and men

Stop Pony Stop

Clippy-tee-clop
Clippy-tee-clop
Hop pony hop
Clippy-tee-clop
Clippy-tee-clop
Stop Pony Stop

Clippy-tee-clop
Clippy-tee-clop
Run pony run
Clippy-tee-clop
Clippy-tee-clop
Stop Pony Stop

Clippy-tee-clop
Clippy-tee-clop
Flop pony flop
Clippy-tee-clop
Clippy-tee-clop
Stop Pony…
Stop.

Dragon Fly

Dragon fly
Flying high
In the sky
So blue

Dragon fly
Come and play
Play with me and stay

Dragon fly
Wings so thin
Tell me please…
Where have you been?

Pretty my Pet

Pretty is my parrot
Pretty is my pet
Pretty pecks pepper
Pretty pecks my thumb
Telling me
Don't forget
To touch me
Your beautiful green pet

Jack Ass

Jack Ass
Yuh carry heavy load

Jack Ass
Yuh calm and gentle

Jack Ass
Yuh help de farmer

Yuh tek him
Ova hill
Eena gully
And On-yah

Jack Ass
Want him grass
From de farmer boss

At Play

Dumplin, Ackee
Yelled Pattee
Let's go
Let's spree

Yippee
Yippee
Shouted all three
Beat us if you can
In our race
To the big, blue sea
The big, blue
Caribbean Sea

The Rainbow Lizard

It slipped in
The rainbow lizard
With tail long and thin
Slipped away
From Adjay
My big brown dog

The rainbow lizard hid
Behind mom's blue dust bin
And caused a din
To chase him out

That Thing

What is that thing?
That follows me
Everywhere I go

What is that thing?
That follows me
Whether I'm fast or slow

What is that thing?
That hides from me
And won't let me see
Its face
But runs with me
In every race

My shadow;
How do you know?

Looking out

From my window, I looked out
Up, around, about
What did I spy?
A clear blue sky
With Mary's little lamb
Floating by

What else did I spy?
Flowers
Yellow, blue, red
Blooming in a square bed

Purple, orange, green
Everywhere could be seen
In butterflies, birds and bees
That flew past the trees
Yes, I did see
Everyone of these

I Love Jesus

I love Jesus
Every day
I Love Jesus
In my work and in my play
I Love Jesus
Whether happy or sad
I Love Jesus
And I'm glad
He came
When I called
Come to me
Sweet Jesus
Come to me and stay

Steps

Poems for 6-9 year olds or Grades 1-3

Lizzie Lizard

Lizzie Lizard took another sip
She sipped and sipped
And said
"This sticks to my lip
I'll need a dip."

On the way
She had a slip
Flip, flip
Went her slip
And got her in a spin
She landed
In a ditch
Where Mousie Mouse
Was cooling
His itchy itch

Mousie Mouse
Very scared
Hid behind a tin
"Lizzie," he squeaked
"What got you that spin?"

Mousie Mouse

Mousie Mouse
Was busy in his house
He ran in
He ran out
He ran up
Running all about
He met Penny Pigeon

Penny Pigeon said he
My house is little
Wee, wee, wee
Come with me
And see

Together in glee
They ran to see
Mouse's house
Called Wee

On their way
That sunny day
They met Piggy Piglet
Playing counting games
One–two–three
Together they went
To see
Mouse's house called Wee

Bertie Bird

Bertie Bird
Flew past by
He was always shy
Stop
Cooed Penny
Stop and see
Mouse's house called Wee

Bertie Bird
Had never heard
Of such a house
For any mouse
In Kee

He stopped to see
Mouse's house
Called Wee
Then went
To tell
His best belle
Bevie Bee

Bevie Bee

Bevie Bee
Couldn't see
Mouse's house
Called Wee

A piece of bread
Hit her head
And she had to flee
Before seeing Wee

She flew real fast
And at last
Met Bernie Butterfly

I have been hit
In my head
By bread
On my way
To Mouse's house
Called Wee
That he built
Out of silt
Here in Kee

Bernie Butterfly

Bernie Butterfly
In his red tie
Went hurriedly to Kee
To see
Mouse's house called Wee

There it stays
Within his gaze
As small as
Small can be
Mouse's house, Wee

Right here
In the land
Of Kee

It would give me pleasure
Said he
To stop and measure
Mouse's House, Wee
But that's a job
For big Bob
And his computer crew

Big Bob

Luckily Big Bob came
With his computer
Game
Name and fame

Mouse's house
He did measure
Plugging in
All the figure

With a hit
His computer lit
Clicked and clicked
But could score
No more
Such tiny figures

Mouse's house
Is wee
It cannot hold his bed
Such small figures
I cannot give
As in my head
They do not live

Mouse's house
Is really wee
I do agree
It's the tiniest thing
Here in Kee

Jahgga, the Janga

Jahgga heard
From Bertie Bird
The very strange story
Of Mouse's house
Wee
He uncovered his head
White and hoary
And shouted out in glory…

I will tell
Of the spell
To shrink Mouse's house
So wee, wee, wee

Dressed his best
He crawled
He rest
To Mouse's house
Wee

I have come
Gurgled he
To clear the mist
Out of this
'Tis not of silt
That it's built
But something
With a dark and gory story

The Happy Three

Ackee, Pattee and Dumplin
Were best, best friends
They played outside
And sometimes inside

Ackee, asked Pattee
Do you have other friends?
Besides me
Let me look
Let me see
Said Ackee

Yes Salt Fish is my main pal
We get together
And have a ball
In and out of season

Pattee, asked Ackee
Who are your special friends?
Well, well said Pattee
They are many…
Beef, Cheese and Chicken
Shrimp and Lobster
Any vegetable you can offer
I'm never ever lonely
With or without you two

Dumplin, asked Ackee and Pattee
Whom do you go out with;
Who sleeps over at your place?
Dumplin stood up stout
And said,
Any one or anything
You can think about.

But for now
Let's forget those friends
Let's stick together

26

Let's play together
Let's have great fun

So Ackee, Pattee, and Dumplin
Held hands
They swayed and danced
They looked real cool
Dancing to their
Favourite Bob Marley tune
Right there by the pool
Baby don't worry about a thing
Every Little Thing will be All Right
All right, all right....

By the Lignum Vitae Tree

Ackee, Pattee
And Dumplin
Ran off his plate
The visitor
Whose nose
Was long and straight

Phew, said Dumplin
I'm glad
We got out
We were almost
Down his throat!

Let's slide
Let's hide
Where we'll
Not be seen

They slowly crept
They slowly crawled
Under the
Lignum vitae tree
There, beside Tastee
Where they could see
Thousands of yellow butterflies
And now and then
A visiting bumble bee

The Good Manners Posse

Pattee had good manners
The best of the three
She would say to Ackee
Thanks for being so kind to me

She'd turn to Dumplin next
And say
Please, please give me a hand
Or, please don't stand
On anyone's feet today

Good morning,
She'd say at the start of the day
Good evening
She'd smile
In her own cute style

Excuse me please
May I lead the way?
Were some more words
Pattee used each day

The others listened well
And soon all three
Became the famous
Good manners posse.

In the Rain

Who can play
In the rain?
Not me
Not me
Said Pattee
I can't play
In the rain

Who can go
In the rain?
Me, me
Said Ackee
I can go in the rain

Who can stay
In the rain?
Me too, me too
Said Dumplin
I can join
Ackee in the rain
    rain, rain
    go away
    that's what Pattee
    likes to say
    go away
    do not stay
    give us time to play
    all day!

Adventurous Pattee

Imagine me
Humble, little Pattee
Taken across the ocean
To 'Merica, Canada and Englan'
Flying across the China Sea
Is my latest spree

Imagine me
Humble, humble Pattee
Missing my best friends
Dumplin and Ackee
Imagine them
Without me

But back to lonely me
Adventurous, ever-present Pattee
Coming from tin pan
A side order now to Choy Fan
Served in China daily
By Jamaican cousins
Of the family
Chinlinpang

Dumplin's Garden Song

Dumplin works in his garden
He works in his garden at home
Dumplin works in his garden
He works in his garden
At home

Dumplin weeds his garden
He weeds his garden at home
Dumplin weeds his garden
He weeds his garden
At home

Dumplin plants his garden
He plants his garden at home
Dumplin plants his garden
He plants his garden
At home

Dumplin sings in his garden
He sings in
his garden at home
Dumplin sings in his garden
He sings his garden
At home

Hoorah, hoorah for Dumplin
And his garden at home
Hoorah, hoorah for Dumplin
And his beautiful garden at home

Ackee's Garden Song

A garden, a garden
Ackee has a garden
She digs it
She weeds it
And plants it up all over

Some flowers,
Some flowers
Ackee has some flowers
She cuts them
And smells them
And then gives them away

Thank you Miss Ackee
Thank you Miss Ackee
We like your flowers
And will use them
To decorate our Teacher's table

Pattee and her Garden

Pattee, Pattee, why have you no garden
I don't know; I don't know
Why I have no garden

Pattee, Pattee, would you like a garden
I don't know; I don't know
If I'd like a garden

Pattee, Pattee should we show you
How to build a garden
I don't know; I don't know
If I'd like to build a garden

Come Pattee, we will show
Then you'll know
How to make a garden
No, No, No
I'd melt like snow
If I try to build a garden

The Rock at the Back

What is that at the back of my yard?
It's a rock at the back of my yard!
What is that on the rock?
At the back of my yard
It's a sock on the rock
At the back of my yard!
What is that on the sock on the rock?
At the back of my yard
It's a lock on the sock, on the rock
At the back of my yard
What is that by the rock at the back of my yard?
It's a cock in a smock with a clock
On the rock at the back of my yard!

All Together

Sunny weather
Rainy weather
Cows give milk
Cows give leather

Sunny weather
Windy weather
Close friends
Play together

Foggy weather
Stormy weather
Hens give eggs
Hens have feather

My Special Friend

My friend Sanjae
Came by me today
We fight together
Our pillows of feather

Sanjae stay
With me tonight
We will play
In the light

Sanjae's so small
She won't grow tall
I love her still
And always will

"Where's Sanjae?"
My sister asks each day
"Right here, at play"
Is my reply
"No", says she
"Give a better try."

She is my friend
You can call it pretend
She's real as real can be
Not to you, just to me.

Birds

Birds, birds everywhere
In the tree
On the ground
In the water
In the air

Little baby birds
Teeny beeny birds
Brother-sister birds
Mother-father bird, birds

Chirping birds
Clucking birds
Quacking birds
Crowing birds
Talking many words birds
Singing all day long birds

Hopping birds
Run along the ground birds
Swimming birds
Diving birds
Flying high in the sky birds
Flying low near the ground birds

Early birds
Dawn chorus –making birds
Noon cruising on the wind birds
Evening say goodbye birds
Lonely night flying
Food fetching birds

Arctic birds
Temperate birds
Tropic plume so bright birds

Black birds
White birds
Yellow, green and blue birds
On the ground
In the water
In the air
Lots and lots of birds
Out there

Prayer Time

I saw it
In his sparkling eye
I saw it
When he turned to cry
I heard it
When he opened his heart
And said
Teach me, Lord the way to go
Teach me Lord, how to show
Your love and kindness
To my friends
Those around me
Those I can
And cannot see
Teach me Lord, your truth
Your honesty, your purity
And most of all-your calm
Lord Jesus,
Teach me how to be
Like you

Big Steps

Poems for 10-12 year olds or Grades 4-6

The Caribbean Region

Chorus
The islands
The islands
The Caribbean islands
I took trip
On a ship
Around the Caribbean

Anguilla and Antigua
Barbados and Barbuda
Cayman, Cuba, Curacao

Chorus
The islands
The islands
The Caribbean islands
I took trip
On a ship
Around the Caribbean

Dominica and Grenada
Guadeloupe, Hispaniola
Jamaica, Martinique and Montserrat

Chorus
The islands
The islands
The Caribbean islands
I took trip
On a ship
Around the Caribbean

Puerto Rico and St. Kitts
St. Lucia and St. Maarten
St. Vincent, Trinidad and Tobago

Chorus
The mainland
The mainland
The Caribbean mainland
I took trip
On a plane
All across the mainland

Belize and Guatemala
Panama, Mexico
And Nicaragua

Chorus
The mainland
The mainland
The Caribbean mainland
I took trip
On a plane
All across the mainland

Columbia and Guyana
Venezuela, Surinam and French Guyana

Chorus
The mainland
The mainland
The Caribbean mainland
I took trip
On a plane
All across the mainland

She

She, they say
Lives in a river
The deepest part of it

She, they told me
Has long horse-tail hair
She spends much time
Combing it

She, they gasped
Is a maiden and a fish
Half and half

She, they say
Soaks up the sun
But is always on the run
From things out side the water

She, they sighed
Is elusive
Rather full of mischief
And you'll never see her
In river, pond or sea
She must be a

_ _ _ _ _ _ _ _ _ _ _ _ _ _

He

He, they say
Is a winner
Always winning
Come what may

He, they say
Is long-legged
Standing, sitting
Running on all eight

He, they say
Will get you
Whether night or day

He, they say
Takes the bigger share
And runs away

He, they say
Is always a man
Never a boy
Never seen with a toy
Never learnt to play
Only to trick
All who dare
To pass his way
He must be

_ _ _ _ _ _ _ _ _ _ _ _ _ _ _

The tricky spider man

Summer Spree

summer came again
long break from school
and learning pain
a hut was built as usual
ready for the big cook-out
cod fish
ripe plantain
flour, butter, oil
mamma gave them from the well-stocked shop
and her consenting, generous smile.

make the fire, that was Jim
Sis' followed orders – flaring flames danced high
the pot is boiling—dash in everything
more wood – it must not stop
more wood – the flame is low
more wood – we must finish quick
stoke the fire – the hut was flat

red flames leapt
blue flames cracked
black pot roared
the hut was gone
food devoured in a flash

The Senses Tell

Look, the river brims
With water
Stop gazing
Look with me, please
 Water, water rushing by
 Catch it; let's try

Listen, birds are singing
In the trees
Stop babbling
Listen with me, please
 Birds, birds in the trees
 You have me stooping on my knees

Feel the cool sea breeze
Stop jumping
Feel with ease, please
 Breeze, breeze blowing free
 All the way to me

Taste mommy's latest bake
Stop slurping
Taste her chocolate cake, please
 Cakes, cakes so sweet
 Oh, so nice to eat

Smell Grandma's curried chicken
Stop snarling
Smell the air with me, please
 Curried chicken, curried chicken
 Nicest thing with dumplin'

PALS

About to begin
We go in
To learn, to know
To do and show
The way to treat another
    Father, friend or brother
    Auntie, grannie, sister, mother
    As a person
    To understand
Not with a magic wand; but
A vow
To save someone from a blow
To help each one to grow
To show another
The better way to go:
    Hold the temper in
    It is a sin
    To strike or tease or hurt;
    To curse and swear
    Is to go against The Father's Will
Wear a smile
Not a frown
Save someone
From going down
    The dark road of shame
    The rough and lonely road of pain
Turn around
Flash that smile
Choose the positive
Refuse the negative;
This is the way to win
This is the way to live

Perky Parrot

Our Environment

This is our environment
Earth is where we live
This is our environment
This is what we plan
To give the Future:
Air that's clean
Water everywhere to be seen
We will blow our steam
And not relent
In our argument
To keep Mother Nature fit and well

This is our environment
Where we have been sent
To live for now
And then endow
Our little world to
A certain future
Not just anyhow
But in a healthy state
So we plan to give:
Much of our time
Even wait in line
For those about
To bring earth hurt
And stop them

This is our environment
This is where we live
This is our environment
One single earth
Land of our birth
One single planet, one big home

From Shame to Fame

In his day
The young boy Bogle
Paul, by first name
Now of hero's fame
Went to church every Sunday
Read his Bible every week day
And learned from the Book of Amos
A lesson most famous
Justice must be allowed to flow like a mighty stream
A brand of justice that was never seen
In St. Thomas where he lived

His piano-keyboard pal
Gordon, by last name
And also of hero's fame
Would often lend
The ear he needed
As he pleaded
His cause
Just treatment of people
In St. Thomas in the East
Where he lived

Together they agreed
The people must be freed
And decided to fight
For their plight
But really made matters worse
Because a bigger force
Under Colonial Crown
Eventually took them down
But their deeds live on

And a century later, man
Made National Heroes
And each a modern fan
Loved, revered
Respected all across the lan'

The little Meuse of Guy's Hill

The spring;
Our Meuse
Was always there
To quench our thirst
To bathe us first
To share our loud outburst
From laughter or from pain
Again and again and again

Ours was a gift of water
To share
To show our care
To people, plant and other living things
Cows, goats, pigs, horses
Invited themselves to it
Drank freely from it
And sometimes chased us from our own legacy

Never drying up
It kept the village green
And often I mused, I was the fairy queen
Who bequeathed the luxury…
A perpetual stream
To my daddy's property

No baptismal font was it
No destroyer of life was it either; it took no one
No sea swelled from its clean, clear water
Half a mile long; no more
A reservoir for rich and poor

Every villager knew its secret head
Its generous flow
And where it mysteriously disappeared
Underground
No one knew where it would eventually go
Children dreaded its depth — the mirrored blue sky
The treacherous glow and slow flow

We respected how far in it to go
At water-fetching or spring-cleaning time

The spring
My daddy's Meuse
The district's name
Began before
And has outlasted *his nine score* and more

The I of the Storm

I am the I of the storm
I set my altitude
I choose my latitude
My course
My rise
My fall

I, the I of the storm
Select my path
My prize
My size
The length of my stay

I am strong
I am furious
I swirl and twirl
I whip and lash
I crash and smash
Leaving lasting legacies behind
I, the I of the storm

I dash waves on waves
I split hills open wide
I gush in gullies
And rage through ravines
To swell streams
Into rivers of frothing foams
Galloping to the sea

I churn the waves
And use their stuffing
To carve new coastlines
I, the I of the storm
I am bold
I am direct,
As I pass
I sweep clean,
I restructure, I remake

And leave a calm
Before and after I hit

I lay lands bare
Yielding to rebirth
New life spawning
On the earth
From fresh rain
I, the I of the storm

I move in
Do my thing
Then move out and about
My own concern
I, the respected
The powerful and feared
Eye of Atlantic Ocean's seasonal storms

My Single Star

I sat at my window
I gazed at the sky
A long steady star-struck gaze
I saw the star
One single bright star
I gazed at the single shining star
It shifted
Left, then right, then left again
And blazed its way
Through the cloud
It's following me!
Leading me—sparkling
Always sparkling
Blinding my gaze
The brilliance appeared
Brighter and brighter and brighter
My single shining shifting star
Steadied itself, dazzled my eyes
I saw a new reality and endless possibility

The Strange Book

In a forgotten corner of a library
Was a little green and gold and black book

The children to the library went
And much time they spent
Reading yellow, red and blue books;
But the little green and gold and black book!
They didn't like its look

They passed it
They poked it
They pushed it
Out of the way
They dropped it
Each and every day

The little green and gold and black book
Got real sad
But tried not to get mad
Just to get into the hand
Of the next child that came its way

It was a happy day when Keisha-Gaye
Strayed away
From her group
The little green and gold and black book
Popped in front of Keisha-Gaye
And whispered, "Take me... today
I'll give you a real treat
For important people in me you'll meet."

Keisha-Gaye took the book
Keisha-Gaye opened the book
Keisha-Gaye shouted out in glee
"This will always belong to me!

It has a magic spell
It teaches me to read
Very well
It has all my friends in it
Doing good deeds
Enjoying themselves
The parties are endless
I can even smell and taste the food
Look!
It shows me people through the ages
It pulls me through its pages
Back into time
I see Nanny as a warrior girl
I see Sam Sharpe in a dizzy whirl
In front of some white people

See Bogle and Gordon there
As little boys
But they have no toys
Oh, they are reading a big black Bible
And reciting Psalm 100
In front of the whole church:"

    Shout for joy to the LORD, all the earth.
    Worship the LORD with gladness;
    Come before him with joyful songs.

    Know that the LORD is God.
    It is he who made us, and we are His
    We are his people, the sheep of his pasture.

    Enter his gates with thanksgiving
    and his courts with praise;
    give thanks to him and praise his name.

    For the LORD is good and his love endures forever;
    His faithfulness continues through all generations.

"It sounds good;
Can you see them fading away?
To become Garvey
Shouting his philosophy

Up you mighty race
Accomplish what you can

So why am I in Beijing
Looking at Asafa, Usain,
Veronica, Melaine and Shelly-Ann?

Oh!
They have accomplished all they can

   The Gold is blinding me

There's not much more that I can take"
"Come this way," said the voice in the
little green and gold and black book
"Take a final look at 1938."

I ran and hugged them tight
Bustamante
and his cousin
Norman Manley!

"What a book
What a trip!"

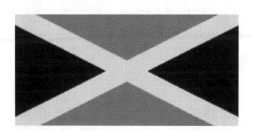

Miss Class

Eena Miss class
Whole heap a t'ings a gwaan
Whole heap a different t'ings a gwaan
But de pickney dem
A learn

Miss give dem game
Miss bring dem fame
Miss fix dem pride
Yuh can tell dat dem feel
Good inside

Miss enlighten dem way
She even turn
Dem night to day
She nuh have to ask
Fi any extra pay
For everybody know
How de slowest pickney dem did stay

All of a sudden
Dem mind open wide
Dem learn fi plan an' decide
Fi solve problem
An t'ink outa box

Miss had to sit this new generation dung
An tell dem how wi came up
Wid de Go,
De Glow
An' de Grow food dem
An convince dem dat it is in their DNA
For it was our ancestors
Who brought plenty of the same food
To de island across the Middle Passage

She had to tell dem dat de power
In our food
Come from de waters
In the belly of Blue Mountain
And de heat from Massa God sun
Plus the knowledge an' fortitude of de folk
Taken by force
Out of Mother Africa
An' left here
Ova three hundred years ago
To make themselves happy and be satisfied
With life in a strange land
As there was no return
To where they came from

Our development might be long and slow
But de food we inherit
Continue to mek we go, grow and glow
Not only in dis island but wherever we go

Sucancobana's Chant

Sucan, Sucan, Sucanco
Sucancobana
That's me; strong, free
Roaming the seven seas
Swaying in tropic breeze
Seeking out the sun
Soaring to the sun
Always on the run
Sucancobana
That's me

I am the season
The right season
Cycles of rebirth
Carnival, festival, Crop over, Trini-lyme
Birthing chamber, christening font
Baptismal stream, Wedding feast, Burial spot
I am Sucancobana, that's me
Strong, free

I am Sucancobana
Asia's claim, Africa's pain
New World's fame, Europe's gain
I populate the land
Plantation, field and single stand
I am Science and Technology
History and Geography
Ecology and Economy
Flora and fauna; all you see
Sucancobana; that's me

I Sucancobana
Am most generous of crops
There all the time
In hut, great house, hospital, hotel
At the match, beach and bar
In the stew, cake and wine
The head, heart and mind

With you in all seasons
Temperate summer, autumn, winter, spring
Tropic hurricane, cyclone, hot, dry, wet weather
Advent, Christmas, Lent and Easter
I'm always the best reason
For the right season
Sucancobana; that's me…strong, free

Downtown Kingston

Have you ever been downtown?
Downtown, Kingston, my friend
Where the push of the cart
And the pick of a pocket
The blare of the horns
And the din of the throng
As they hurry along
In endless flurry
To buy or sell
Makes you wonder
Or worry
About ending up in hell?

Have you ever been downtown?
Downtown, Kingston, my friend
Where your smell can tell
Of seeping sewer
Going out to sea
And your ears deafen
From vendors yelling out the plea

Come, buy from me;
This only for a dollar
This for two
See, it was waiting jus' for you.

Have you ever been downtown?
Downtown, Kingston, my friend
And see a lawyer–dressed in black
Or a doctor–dressed in white
A banker–all in grey
A hairdresser in the way
A merchant looking out
On the man he paid to shout

Come inside
Check it out
Man marina… from $50.00
Homan skirt … from $50.00
Pickney shoes… from $90.00

Or a teacher
A Preacher
Politician, 'lectrician
Police or DJ
Making their way
Up or down a street
Parade, park or lane
Yes, my friend Tajae
Downtown is all this and more
Downtown is a call, a fall
A lure.

Thanks and Praises

Thank you Father for this new day
Thank you for the blessings it's bringing my way
Thank you for waking me up
For filling my cup
For keeping me warm
And away from harm
Thank you for the friends I'll meet
And all who'll greet
Me as I go to praise
*   The mountains*
*   And the hills*
*   The heat and the chills*
*   The forests and the seas*
*   The people, birds and bees*
*   The history, heritage and land*
*   To praise everything and take my stand*